John A. Macdonald

P.B. Waite

Fitzhenry & Whiteside Limited

Contents

THE CANADIANS
A Continuing Series

John A. Macdonald

Author: P. B. Waite
Design: Kerry Designs
Cover Illustration: John Mardon

Canadian Cataloguing in Publication Data
Waite, P. B. (Peter Busby), 1922-
John A. Macdonald
(The Canadians) Rev. ed.
Includes bibliographical references and index.
ISBN 1-55041-479-8

1. Macdonald, John A. (John Alexander), Sir, 1851-1891.   2. Prime ministers – Canada – Biography – Juvenile literature. 3. Canada – Politics and government – 1867-1914 – Juvenile literature. I. Title. II. Series

FC521.M3W32 1999   971.05'1'092   C99-932550-7

© 1999 Fitzhenry & Whiteside Limited
195 Allstate Parkway, Markham, Ontario L3R 4T8

Chapter 1
Macdonald, the Man

If you had met John A. Macdonald you might not have been that impressed. He was tall and had curly black hair; there was that much to be said on the positive side. He was not really ugly, but he was certainly not much to look at either. Perhaps that is what gave him his charm. All beauty can be a source of corruption for its possessors; it is so obviously a form of power. Macdonald had to seek his power by other means. He had a ploughed, plain face, with a blaze of blue eyes and an irredeemably large nose. His nose was irresistible. Cartoonists loved him for it. It gave him an air, as one French Canadian said, at once mocking and artless, as if you were never quite sure whether he were serious or not.

He was rather a man's man, a man for evenings over whisky and talk with a few cronies. He knew, and he gathered, stories from all sides of life, some decidedly racy; after a few drinks he could get up and mimic a local preacher with devastating accuracy, sending his friends into roars of laughter. He had seen quite a bit of life as a lawyer. One of his first clients was hanged in Kingston for leading a foray into Canada from the United States in 1838. Von Schoultz's case was hopeless from the start, but Macdonald was impressed with the man. The things he had admired in Von Schoultz – his character, his toughness, his range of experience – were to be Macdonald's too. Macdonald had a broad sense of humor; there was precious little that was sacred. He always read widely in biography, history, literature, where a great many of his stories came from. He remembered what he read, the way he would remember your name and face, apparently without effort. It just seemed to sort itself out, easily and naturally, in that capacious mind of his.

One obvious source of his political power was his way of remembering those whom he had met. He

Lord Dufferin

Miles Gustav von Schoultz

would not only remember you, but your wife and children and even your problems. It is not as easy as it seems. One Nova Scotian politician tried it. Going up to a constituent whom he had not seen for a couple of years, he said, "And how is your father now, Mr. Brownlee?" "He's still dead," said the outraged Mr. Brownlee. No, you had to be right on such matters. Macdonald was also good at what Canadians used to call "soft sawder," what we would call buttering people up. This applied even to Governors General who, though often men of sophistication and experience, were human like anyone else. Lord Dufferin, the Governor General of Canada from 1872 to 1878, was given an Ll.D. from McGill about 1873, and Macdonald and some of his cabinet went down to Montreal for it. On the way back in the train, Hector Langevin, Macdonald's Minister of Public Works, read a report in the Montreal paper that Lord Dufferin, in his convocation address to McGill, spoke Greek without the slightest error in pronunciation or grammar. "Great heavens," said Langevin to Macdonald, "how on earth did the reporter know that?" "I told him," said Macdonald. "But," said Langevin, "you don't know any Greek." "That is quite right," Macdonald replied, "but I know something about politics."

Macdonald was capable of refusing a request with more charm than some people used in granting one. One supporter of his wanted a particular job rather badly, and came to Ottawa to see Macdonald about it. After the usual inquiries after the man's wife and family, Macdonald asked what he could do for him, and when he learned what the man wanted, looked at him for a minute, as if impressed with the man's transcendent ability and intelligence. "Why," said the Prime Minister, "why on earth would a man like you want a paltry job like that? It's not good enough for you. Just you wait a while, and we'll find you something much better." Flattered by Sir John's estimate of his great talents, the man decided to wait. He had to wait a long time, for nothing quite good enough

Macdonald, the Man

for him ever came along.

You could say, that is not quite a decent thing for Macdonald to do. And you would be right. Politics is apt to be like that. "He is *such* a dodger," said one friend of Macdonald's who knew him all too well. He was a difficult man to pin down. He hated being forced into a corner. He liked room for maneuver. So he was a dodger, and an artful one at that. He believed that not much good was done by being in a hurry. A lot of things that people thought were desperately urgent were frequently nothing of the kind. Most issues could be put off, frequently with profit to all concerned. Not a few of them, having been put off, will disappear altogether. A little procrastination was a good thing; Macdonald might even have said, the more the better. This attitude grew as he became older, until by the 1880's it had become almost a vice. It sometimes exasperated his colleagues, always to be putting off until tomorrow what you might otherwise have decided to do today. This does not mean Macdonald was lazy. He wasn't. But he did not get the name "Old Tomorrow" for nothing.

Macdonald around 1877

Macdonald always used to say you caught more flies with honey than with vinegar. Of course, he could be sharp on occasion, especially when crossed, for he had a temper. He would not be put upon. "Skin your own skunks," he once put as a peremptory postscript in a letter to a young cabinet minister who wanted something outrageous, as cabinet ministers not infrequently did. But Macdonald's instinct most of the time was the other way. In the House of Commons he was solicitous in supporting his own followers. He would never do what the Liberal leader Edward Blake used to do, sleep through a speech by a member of his own party. Macdonald would pay attention, or pretend to pay attention, interjecting a "hear, hear" even to some awful platitude that the House had heard dozens of times before, just to let his supporters know, and the House know, that the leader of the party was listening, however dull the speech might be. Sometimes when the speech was over, if the House was breaking up to go home for the night, Macdonald would go to the speaker and tell him what a wonderful speech it was, and in a voice loud enough to be heard by everyone else. Political loyalties are often built upon outrageous hypocrisy of exactly this kind.

Macdonald also believed in being friendly with members of the Opposition. You never knew when they might decide to come over, and Macdonald tried to make it easy for them to do so. Not many did, but nevertheless he had a following even on the Liberal side of the House. David Thompson, the Liberal member for Haldimand County, Ontario, from before Confederation until he died, had been away part of one session in the early 1880's on account of illness. Upon his return to Ottawa, the first man he met was the leader of his party, Edward Blake. Blake gave him a pleasant nod. A few minutes later Thompson came upon Sir John Macdonald. Macdonald did not just nod. He went up to Thompson, clapped him on the shoulder, and said, "Well! Davie, old man, it's good to see you back! I hope you are better and that you'll live to vote against me many a day yet, as you've always done!" "Hang it all," said Thompson afterward, "if it doesn't go against the grain to give votes in support of Edward Blake or Sir Richard Cartwright and to vote against a man like Sir John!"

It was these qualities of heart, as well as of mind, that made Sir John Macdonald great. He had to a nicety the common touch. He could be stiff and dignified when he chose to be; you could not take liberties with him, for that was something he was liable to take ill; but clearly he enjoyed life and somehow helped to make others around him do the same. Many liked him, though not everyone trusted him. The Liberals did not, especially after the Pacific Scandal that broke in 1873, but they retained an admiration, sometimes grudgingly conceded, for his talent and his spirit. These had made him into the man he was, and gave him the greatness that was, and is rightly his. That is really what this book is about.

Chapter 2
Kingston and Glenora

John A. Macdonald was born in Glasgow, Scotland, on January 10, 1815. His father was Hugh Macdonald, who came from the northeast coast, north of Inverness, from the town of Dornach. He had migrated to Glasgow to make his fortune. Hugh Macdonald was a pleasant, easy-going man, fond of friends, talk and drink. He was ambitious enough, but woefully lacking the persistence necessary to realize ambitions. Always looking for something better, he usually succeeded in making things worse. His mother, Helen Shaw, was made of sterner stuff. She came from the Spey valley, South of Inverness, a valley of rolling farms, upland pastures, good crops, and Scotch whisky. She had brains, capacity, and persistence. Probably Hugh Macdonald's marriage to her represented his instinctive need for someone capable; what the advantage was on her side is less certain. They were married about 1811 and within eight years five children were born; the eldest died, and John Alexander was the remaining eldest and finally the only son. Hugh Macdonald began to despair of success in Glasgow; things had gone from the not-so-bad to the not-so-good (his little firm made cotton bandannas), and hearing from relations in Kingston, Upper Canada, that things might be better there, Hugh Macdonald, his wife and four children, all sailed for Canada early in the summer of 1820. They arrived in Kingston in mid July, their son John Alexander just over five years old. Young John's impressions of Scotland became hazy; he was going to be, in most essential respects, a home-grown Canadian.

Kingston was a small, prosperous town, at the corner of Lake Ontario where the St. Lawrence begins its long run to the sea. It was stone-built, and not unlike the stone-built Scottish towns from which the family had come. Hugh Macdonald decided to stay in Kingston.

Macdonald was probably born on this street, Brunswick Place, in Glasgow, although we cannot be entirely certain.

Kingston in the 1820's. Many Canadian politicians in Canada's early history had a Scottish background.

He was no pioneer. He had been brought up in Dornach as a shop-keeper's son, and that was what he was, even though his ambition always kept reminding him that he was destined for bigger things than shops. This ambition kept him moving from shop to shop, until finally, in 1825, they took possession of the Stone Mills, at Glenora, some forty-five kilometres west of Kingston, overlooking the Adolphus Reach, a lovely stretch of water that ran northward and westward up to the Bay of Quinte. The milling business was not a great success either, but it never actually failed, and with Helen Shaw Macdonald's help, they remained there for about ten years.

That was where Macdonald and his sisters really grew up, the place they thought of as home. It was a good place to be. To the very last he loved the Reach and the Bay of Quinte, the hills and woods of Glenora, with their views along the lade toward Kingston, or northward toward Napanee. It was country meant for young boys with an urge to ramble and explore in the long summers. In the longer winters, however, Macdonald was sent, at some cost to the family, to school in Kingston. Belief in education is an old Scots tra-dition, and Helen Macdonald was going to make sure her son was educated as well as possible. It was not easy on young Macdonald either. He had to board in Kingston, and this meant long separa-tions from family and home. It was true that home was only forty-five kilometres away, but it might as well have been one hundred and

forty-five for all the good it did, transportation being awkward and expensive. However, he had cousins in Kingston, the MacPhersons, and he was there often, and had access to their library. He began to read, in a constantly widening range. He was to read all his life, and by the time he was fifty, the time of Confederation, he had an extraordinarily well-stocked mind. And he was lucky in other ways. The District Grammar School at Kingston was good, in a province where bad schools were numerous. He got a solid grounding in arithmetic, mathematics, Latin and French with two masters who were exceptionally able.

By the end of the year 1829, young Macdonald's schooling was over for good. His parents could not afford to send him to university; what universities there were, were a long way away in 1830, in Montreal, in Fredericton or Halifax. Macdonald later said that if he had gone to university, he would have ended up in literature, not in politics. He was now nearly fifteen years old, and it was time to consider a career. He was articled to a Kingston lawyer, George Mackenzie, passed his entrance examination for articling at Toronto (where he went by boat), and settled in Kingston to learn the law by doing it.

Mackenzie's legal business prospered, as did Kingston, and about 1832 he set up a branch office in Napanee, some forty kilometres to the west; young Macdonald was given the job of running it. At this

Isabella Clark Macdonald

stage Macdonald was still quiet, bookish and reserved, though efficient. He would not have been given the job but for his aptitude, something which he seems to have got from his mother rather than his father. The gregarious and fun-loving side of his nature, which came from his father, was still developing. In this respect he was probably what we call now a "late developer," his intellectual maturity being well in advance of his social. It was at Napanee, however, where this latter side of him ripened handsomely. He liked company, he was good at telling anecdotes, and as his confidence grew he got better at it. Soon he was mimicking his elders outrageously. He had by now taken over another law practice near Picton, when his patron, George Mackenzie, died of cholera in Kingston. Mackenzie was in church on a Sunday morning, and was dead on Monday morning, in August of 1834. By the next summer Macdonald had moved to Kingston to set up his own practice among friends, acquaintances, business associates there, and was admitted to the Bar early in 1836, at the age of twenty-one.

Macdonald's practice went well, and he was able, early in 1842, to cross the wintry Atlantic to see something of England and Scotland. His father had died in September 1841 and there were legal questions in Scotland to be cleared up. Macdonald had a good time; his letters from London show him in remarkably good form. He even bought himself a substantial library and arranged to have it shipped from Chancery Lane to Kingston, Upper Canada. Still, as he wrote his mother, holidays were not everything. "To a person obligated all his life to be busy, idleness is not pleasure." That may have been for his mother's benefit, for he was still in England a month later. He visited relatives in the Isle of Man, and there met his half-cousin, Isabella Clark, who charmed him and promised to come out to visit mutual relatives in Kingston next year.

She came out in the summer of 1843. Within a few weeks of her arrival, she and Macdonald were married, on September 1, 1843, in St. Andrew's Church. He was twenty-eight years old, she thirty-four. Isabella (or Isa as Macdonald used to call her) was a lady of poise and considerable charm; she had a quiet splendor about her. She seemed to radiate a kind of sweetness that lifted the heart without cloying the senses. Macdonald was very much in love with her. They moved into a house on Brock Street, Kingston. It was now to be the base for the young married lawyer beginning a successful career.

Macdonald's bachelor home on Rideau Street, Kingston

Kingston was a Scottish, Presbyterian and Conservative town, and in about that order of priority. When Macdonald went into politics, therefore, he went in on the Conservative side, but he had seen enough of politics from Kingston not to believe slavishly in the politics of Tory Toronto. There were many things wrong that needed correction, as the rebellions of 1837 had shown.

Kingston had been selected as the capital of the united province of Canada, created in 1841 by the union of Upper Canada and Lower Canada. Macdonald was elected to the Province of Canada Assembly in the election of October 1844, for Kingston. In that year the capital was moved to Montreal, and it was there, on November 28, 1844, that he first took his seat in a legislative body. Though he was to be out of office several times, he was in fact never to be out of a legislature during the rest of his life.

Chapter 3
In Politics, 1844-1857

Macdonald's political career began well. He soon became the Receiver General (the chief collector of revenue) in the Conservative government of W.H. Draper, in May 1847. He was not in office long, however, before he began to feel the Draper administration was not going to last much longer, and by the general election of December 1847 he believed the government would be defeated. He was right. In March 1848 it resigned on a want of confidence motion in the House. The Draper regime was no more, and the Reform government of Baldwin and Lafontaine came into power. Macdonald was now out of office and would remain so until 1854.

Macdonald's law office in Kingston. Without his law practice, Macdonald would have been unable to remain in politics.

He now needed his law practice to live on. In 1843 he had taken as partner, Alexander Campbell, who looked after things when Macdonald was away. Macdonald got two-thirds of the profits and Campbell one-third. Increasingly, as time went on, Campbell became restless and resentful with this arrangement, especially after Macdonald took office in May 1847, and could no longer do much of the firm's business. Campbell felt he was doing most of the work, and Macdonald was drawing most of the profit. Macdonald also had rather casual business habits, including that of using the firm's current income to pay election expenses or buy land. By 1848

Campbell wanted out, and despite Macdonald's willingness to split the profits fifty-fifty, at Campbell's insistence they split up. Macdonald was never to be lucky in his law partners. His next partner, A.J. MacDonnell, whom he took in 1854, lasted ten years, and when he died left Macdonald with enormous debts.

By the end of the 1840s Macdonald had more than his share of personal troubles. About a year after their marriage Isabella began to be ill. She was eventually to become an invalid. With infinite difficulty Macdonald managed to get her south as far as Georgia in the autumn of 1845. There she remained when he returned to Canada just after New Year's, 1846, to attend both his law practice and Parliament. Isabella remained in the south, and they were reunited only at Christmas 1846, in New York. Then, still in the United States, in August 1847 she gave birth to a boy, a long and difficult delivery, that virtually prostrated her. Even then Macdonald had to leave her after a few days to get back to Montreal. He was Receiver General and his colleagues in cabinet and in his department needed him. His consolation was that the new baby boy was healthy. His wife definitely was not, but she came back to Kingston in the summer of 1848, and the little family was reunited. By now Macdonald was out of office, and he could truly be a family man again.

He wanted to move them all to more secluded surroundings. Bellevue House was selected on the outskirts of Kingston. The rent would be heavy; he would have to have servants; but it was quiet and

Bellevue House, Kingston

Hugh John Macdonald in later life. Hugh John followed his father into politics and became Premier of Manitoba in 1900.

pleasant, an Italian-style villa that Macdonald sometimes called the Pekoe Pagoda after its slightly fantastic architecture.

There he sought to nurse his wife back to health. But the year-old boy died and Isabella, despite some periodic rallies, did not really improve. But she delivered another boy in March 1850, who did live, and was to live rather a long time, to become ultimately Sir Hugh John Macdonald (1850-1929); Isabella, however, was never really healthy again. Macdonald's letters are full of her; how he nursed those fragile hopes of her improvement! Week to week, month to month, manifestly he was determined to look upon the bright side of things. It was not easy. On a typical evening he would be downstairs entertaining company, perhaps with the help of a servant, and Isabella would be a world away, upstairs in bed, the permanent invalid. In these years as a quasibachelor, and in later years as a real widower, Macdonald learned to drink, and to drink hard, perhaps as a refuge from this lonely life, perhaps because he enjoyed the good fellowship that went with it.

Isabella continued to live; Macdonald brought her to Toronto, when the capital of the Province of Canada was moved there in 1855, so that they could spend the winters of 1855-56, and 1856-57, together. But in the spring of 1857 she went back to Kingston, and in that autumn she stayed there. By Christmas she was dying; Macdonald, in the middle of a general election, managed to get home to her by train on Christmas night. She died three days later. He was left with a seven-year-old son, and memories of fourteen years of a sad, limp, disjointed marriage.

For many men all of this could have turned their lives into shipwreck. Macdonald's navigation was of sterner stuff. There was a resilience, a toughness of moral fibre in him that seems to have come from his mother. Later in life, when people complained to him about troubles, he used to say, "Do you expect to go through life without troubles? If you do, you have been deceived. Troubles come as naturally to man as sparks fly upward from a fire." He believed that you could not allow your life to be dragged down by difficulties; everyone has them, so you had better learn to live with them. He had even, in 1856, felt it necessary to challenge a certain Colonel Arthur Rankin to a duel as a result of certain remarks Rankin had made in the Assembly. Since Macdonald was the chief law officer of the government, a duel would have had to be fought outside the province, but Macdonald was quite prepared for that. As it turned out, Rankin admitted his remarks were unjust, and the duel never came off. But the unwritten code was that a man could not refuse a duel without being labeled a coward, unless, as in Rankin's case, he had clearly been in the wrong and chose to apologize.

By 1857 Macdonald had become in fact the Premier of the Province of Canada. He had always believed that the days of unregenerate Conservatism had been numbered; the defeat of the Draper government in 1848 had confirmed him in that view. In 1854 the Reform government of Francis Hincks and A.N. Morin, the successor to the great party of Baldwin and Lafontaine, broke in two. In effect what happened, after the election of that summer, was that the Conservative party of Canada West joined with A.N. Morin in forming what was called a Liberal-Conservative government, under the nominal leadership of Sir Allan MacNab. The real architect of the change was John A. Macdonald.

Top: Sir Allan MacNab

The name of this new group was important. Macdonald always believed the Conservative party needed some progressive or liberal leading edge. Like the leading edge of a wing, it gave lift to Conservative politics, and prevented the party from sinking to the ground under the weight of its own inertia.

In 1855 George Etienne Cartier arrived on the scene. He was a short, tough, mastiff-like man, who had been something of a rebel in 1837, something of a poet, and now like many French Canadians had moved to the right, and was a corporation lawyer in Montreal. Macdonald and Cartier were soon close friends and colleagues. They realized that they each needed the other. They were to remain allies for a long time to come, in fact until Cartier's death in May 1873. (They had some strains to endure, notably in 1867, when Lord Monck, the Governor General, was so foolish as to arrange for a knighthood for Macdonald and none for Cartier. That was not Macdonald's fault, and fortunately, Cartier realized it; the omission was remedied, pretty much on Macdonald's insistence.) By the autumn of 1857 Macdonald was the Premier of the Province, and Cartier was his right-hand man from Canada East.

Bottom: George Etienne Cartier

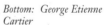

Chapter 4
The Double Shuffle and After, 1857-1864

The New York stock market crash of 1857 affected Canada severely, and governments in power do not do well in bad times. One of Macdonald's close Conservative associates, John Hillyard Cameron, lost everything he had by the failure of a New York brokerage firm, and was plunged into debt. Cameron lost, it is estimated, $500,000. (Multiply by about ten to get current equivalents.) He proposed to pay back every cent he owed. He tried. He'd paid off over half of it when he died in 1876, but his estate still owed $200,000. Of course in the nineteenth century (and well on into the twentieth) life was a good deal more precarious, in all kinds of ways. Macdonald, who was certainly not a speculator on the scale of John Hillyard Cameron, was nevertheless to get into trouble a decade later. His law partner, A.J. MacDonnell, died in 1864 and then, as now, you were liable for all the debts of both yourself and your partner. MacDonnell had been very inefficient and careless, but it was not until 1869 that Macdonald discovered the extent of this bad management; he actually owed the Merchant's Bank something like $80,000. Instead of being worth $100,000 or so, as he thought, he was in debt. He mortgaged all the property he had, borrowed $3000 from a friend, and started all over again. This at the age of fifty-four, when most men have well in hand most of the goods of the world they are going to acquire.

The firm of Macdonald and Cartier also had a hard fight in the December general elections of 1857. The sectional lines of the Province of Canada were showing signs of hardening. Each half of the province had been given an equal number of representatives in the Act of Union of 1841. In the early years of the Union, Canada East had a much larger population than Canada West, and, in fact, it had been deliberately under-represented. By 1855, however, it was the other way around, and Canada West did *not* like it. It wanted all the representatives in Parliament it felt it was entitled to by its population. The rallying cry was just that: "rep. by pop.", that is representation by population. Thus it was becoming more difficult to justify to Canada West, for example, legislation like the Separate School Act of 1855, that had been approved by only a minority of the repre-

Macdonald around 1856

sentatives from Canada West. Nonetheless, with
Cartier, Macdonald was still in power. They pulled
themselves together and met the new session of
Parliament that opened in Toronto on
February 25, 1858.

It was a long, cranky, awkward session.
The opposition defeated the government
on July 31, over whether Ottawa ought to
be the new capital of the province. It did
not matter that the decision about
Ottawa had already been made by the
Queen on recommendations from
Canada. The elements that did not
want Ottawa combined to bring down
the government, which thus resigned in
a nice patriotic flourish, defending the
Queen's decision.

The two principal leaders of the
opposition, George Brown and Antoine-
Aimé Dorion, formed a government; they
were actually in power two days, and then
they, too, went down to defeat in the House
of Assembly. Cartier and Macdonald obligingly came back again. Macdonald began to
taunt the erstwhile Brown-Dorion government –
and he could be positively infuriating at that game
– by calling them "Her Majesty's Most Ephemeral
Administration." Since Macdonald and Cartier, by
means of a fast bit of legal trickery, managed to avoid having to go for by-elections, and Brown and Dorion had had to, this

George Brown (above)

teasing by Macdonald was rubbing salt into wounds. Brown found it
nearly impossible to forgive the Conservatives for this iniquitous
"double shuffle," as the Toronto *Globe* was soon calling it. Even the
Governor General did not escape the wrath of Brown and his paper
for permitting it, and Sir Edmund Head was freely damned with the
rest of the government.

Nevertheless, the Cartier-Macdonald government would remain
in power until 1862. One important addition was made to it; that
was Alexander Galt. Galt was a business man from Sherbrooke, a
successful railway entrepreneur, and something of a financial wizard.
He was also, unlike many business men, something of a romantic in
politics, continually dreaming up projects and ideas that were years
ahead of their time. One of these peculiar ideas was the
Confederation of all the British North American colonies. Cartier

Alexander Tilloch Galt (left)

The Double Shuffle and After, 1857-1864

U.S.President Abraham Lincoln

and Macdonald needed Galt, but they probably felt they could get along without Confederation. But since Galt insisted upon Confederation as a condition of his joining the government, then Cartier and Macdonald would put the best face on it they could. They did not like Confederation much, but if Galt thought he could do anything with it, let him go ahead.

He did not, indeed could not, do much. He tried. Letters were sent off to Newfoundland, Prince Edward Island, Nova Scotia, New Brunswick about Confederation. In 1858 Galt and Cartier and another colleague even went to England about it. But this Canadian initiative for Confederation ended up a failure. It aroused little response in the Atlantic colonies and none at all in London. Gradually the issue was dropped, and for the time being was not revived.

Then, in the spring of 1861, came the American Civil War. Despite all that Abraham Lincoln could do to assure the Southern states that neither he nor his Republican Party meant to abolish slavery, the South refused to believe him. Given the statements of some Republicans, the South's reluctance was understandable. Thus, immediately after the election of Lincoln, in November, 1860, the United States began slowly to come apart. The bombardment of the U.S. federal fort in Charleston harbour in April, 1861, by Southern artillery was the beginning of a long and terrible struggle that would transform the North and South into two armed camps. British North Americans could only look on in amazement and apprehension, and as the war got bloodier, with horror.

It was not peaceful in Mexico either. The French invaded Mexico in 1862 with some British support and more encouragement, to collect debts; the French stayed on, conquered the Mexicans, and set up an Emperor with a court, in Mexico City. They soon found themselves in trouble. The Emperor, Maximilian, was well-meaning enough, but the Mexican people found the whole regime intolerable;

a revolution broke out, and it was to end in June 1867, with the court-martial and execution of Maximilian by Juarez, the revolutionary leader. Well, might a French-Canadian paper say with some feeling, the peaceful years of North America were over, and the era of militarism had begun.

And the British got into it, or they nearly did. In November 1861, a British mail steamer, R.M.S. *Trent*, travelling peacefully between Havana, Cuba, and London, was stopped on the high seas by a United States warship, and two Confederate agents, in civilian clothes, were forcibly taken off. The British had little enough sympathy with the North anyway; but this was too much. The British Prime Minister, Lord Palmerston, stormed into a cabinet meeting in London, flung the despatch on the table, and said, "I don't know whether you will stand for this, but I am damned if I will." Off went a stiff despatch to Washington; off went 11 000 British troops to reinforce the British garrisons in British North America – in Halifax, Saint John, Fredericton, Quebec, Ile-aux-Noix, Montreal, Kingston and Toronto. The United States had the sense to back down. As Lincoln said, "One war at a time is enough." The United States returned the two Southern agents who were allowed to proceed to Britain.

So the *Trent* crisis passed. Or so many Canadians were pleased to think. When the Cartier-Macdonald government tried to

Headquarters of the Army of the Potomac, 1864

appropriate $500,000 in May 1862 to strengthen the Canadian militia, it was defeated in the Assembly. So Cartier and Macdonald resigned once more, again on a patriotic note. But this time they did not return so quickly. Not in fact for two years. In the meantime this defeat of the Militia Bill of 1862 made the British as angry at the Canadians as they had been at the Americans six months before. In November 1861, Britain had, at great expense, undertaken to reinforce Canada with British troops. Now, here were the Canadians unwilling to spend a paltry $500,000 to defend themselves! As the London *Spectator* put it, in July, 1862, "It is, perhaps, our duty to defend the Empire at all hazards; it is not part of it to defend men who will not defend themselves." There were other reasons for the Canadian defeat besides that ignominious imputation. But nevertheless, Canadian stock was never lower in Britain than in the mid-1860's, when the crisis with the United States was growing worse, owing to a series of events, from the depredations of Southern warships like the *Alabama* (built in England), to raids by Confederates from British North America into the United States.

The Alabama *had been built in a famous Liverpool, England, shipyard without much attempt at concealment other than the fact that she had a number, 290, not a name. The British had been warned she was intended as a Confederate sea raider, but British sympathies toward the South persuaded them to look the other way until it was too late. She got to sea in 1862 and for two years wreaked havoc with Northern shipping, until she was finally sunk near Cherbourg, by a Northern warship in 1864.*

Thus when Macdonald and Cartier came back into power, in April 1864 (the government was actually called the Taché-Macdonald administration) there had accumulated a formidable bill of problems with the United States. And the internal difficulties of governing the Province of Canada effectively had steadily grown worse. In fact, it was now nearly impossible. There had been three different governments in less than two years; and on June 14, 1864, the Taché-Macdonald government was defeated in the Assembly, by two votes. What to do? There had been an election in 1863, and it had changed nothing. A new election probably would make no difference. Had the Canadians come to the end of their resources? Where could they go? The answer was to be... Confederation.

Chapter 5
Confederation, 1864 - 1867

U p to this point Macdonald had done very little about Confederation. He had talked about it in 1861 in ways that suggested his views had shifted from his negative attitude in 1858. But still, even in 1864, Confederation was for him of little practical significance. And, for Macdonald, issues that had little practical significance were dead, or at best they were only potentially alive, in the womb of the future, so to speak, the gestation period being anyone's guess. So it should be a matter of no surprise that Macdonald opposed Confederation right down to the end, right down to the defeat of the Taché-Macdonald government in June 1864.

Then things changed. George Brown, the leader of the Reform Party, who had at his command some 35 seats in the 130-seat Assembly, offered a coalition to Macdonald to carry Confederation. Brown had opposed Macdonald for over a decade. He had developed the Reform Party of Canada West and had fought the Liberal-Conservatives ever since 1854. He had been Premier for two days in the ill-starred government in 1858. But he had come some distance from the somewhat irascible and noisy partisan of those days. He had married, for one thing. In November 1862, a bachelor of forty-four, Brown had fallen in love with Anne Nelson, of Edinburgh, Scotland, while there on a visit, had married her, and brought her to Toronto. Diseases that come late in life are apt to be severe, and love is no different. Much of what we know about some of the inside details of Confederation is because George Brown was so in love with Anne that he hated being away from her; and he wrote her letters, sometimes two or three a day. They now had a baby of whom Brown was excessively fond. He was altogether

A memorial statue of Macdonald in Kingston

a more accommodating man than the Brown of 1858. His offer to Macdonald to help realize Confederation was magnanimous and statesmanlike. Brown never did a nobler deed.

For Macdonald, Cartier, and the Premier, Sir Etienne Taché, this offer of a coalition changed everything. It put Confederation on a plane, not of after-dinner grandiloquence, or newspaper editorials, but on a plane of politically realizable possibilities. It meant the practicality of Confederation, at least as far as the Province of Canada was concerned. The coalition was composed of three of the four main political groups in the province. Whatever it chose to sponsor could command three-quarters of the votes in the Legislative Assembly. Of course it meant taking some risks. For the French-Canadian ministers, Cartier, Taché, Langevin and others, it was a bold step, and they had to take their courage in their hands. Fortunately for them, they did not need to have an election until 1867; they could go ahead, trusting their own judgment, and trusting that a sufficient majority of their electorate would, in the end, support them.

Macdonald and his colleagues spent the summer of 1864 formulating a concrete proposal to put to the Maritime provinces. It was hard, though interesting work, but it was not all sweetness and light. Macdonald arrived at one of the last Canadian cabinet meetings, August 28, 1864, three hours late and half drunk. Before the busi-

ness was well in hand he was drunk on the beer that he had with his lunch. He also became quarrelsome, and brought up an old argument with Brown over the contracts for the Parliament Buildings. Finally Galt had to settle the quarrel, and even then Macdonald swore his friends had betrayed him and he would resign forthwith. He didn't. But he could get like that sometimes. Finally, they all set off together, in gorgeous weather, by steamer for Charlottetown, arriving there on Thursday, September 1, 1864.

The Canadians at Charlottetown carried things in great style. It was rather a *coup de théâter*, as the French say, steaming into Charlottetown aboard their ship, the *Queen Victoria*, and almost at once winning the Conference over to their side. The Maritime provinces had their own difficulties of course, but none of them had a fraction of the problems that Canada had. The three Maritime electorates had no particular desire to change things. But some of the Maritime politicians were more restless, and could see advantages in Confederation. These men provided the dynamism, the leadership and the courage, that made possible the substantial acceptance of the Canadian proposals at the Charlottetown Conference. The Canadians had been extremely lucky. They had come well prepared, both with wine in the hold and practical proposals on the bridge. But none of this would have had much result had the spirit been lacking. So the Canadians, with wine and champagne, and a splendid

Delegates to the Charlottetown Conference—Macdonald is seated at center.

Macdonald in the formal attire befitting his title, 1884

vision of what might really be done, swept all obstacles aside. Some of the Maritime politicians were never the same again; they were converted to the dream, the hope, of a great new nation in North America, made from colonial materials, *a mari usque ad mare*. What the Charlottetown Conference started, the Quebec Conference largely finished. Macdonald had an important part to play. While he was not the chairman of the Quebec Conference (Sir Etienne Taché was, as Premier of Canada), he had had a great deal to do with shaping the form of the Quebec Resolutions, which was the main document to come out of that Conference. Macdonald himself was not altogether happy about a federal constitution for British North America, but it was clear that the French Canadians, and the Prince Edward Islanders, would insist upon it, and the federal idea also had some limited support in New Brunswick and Nova Scotia. So it was called "federal." But Macdonald, and others, who did not want to leave too much power in the hands of the future provinces, tried to arrange things so that the new central government to be established at Ottawa, would be strong enough to overcome the divisive forces so clearly at work in the American Civil War. The new constitution for British North America was called "federal" all right, but Macdonald did not really care what it was *called*. He was interested in what it *was*. As far as he was concerned that meant concentrating as much power as possible at the center, with the proposed Dominion government.

Of course the Quebec Conference also had its social, as well as its constitutional side. If British North America needed a new constitution, it appeared as if the delegates were going to need new constitutions too. It was work most of the day and partying most of the night. The Governor General's sister-in-law reported on Thursday, October 20:

John A. Macdonald is always drunk now, I am sorry to say, and when some one went to his room the other night, they found him in his night shirt, with a railway rug thrown over him, practicing Hamlet before a looking-glass.

But by then the worst problems of the conference were nearly over. Perhaps Macdonald had some justification for practising Hamlet!

The actual story of how Confederation was carried, in the Province of Canada, in Nova Scotia, New Brunswick, its fate in Newfoundland and in Prince Edward Island, is a fascinating one that has been told many times. The Canadian coalition held together through all the difficulties. Though Brown resigned toward the end of 1865, his support for Confederation continued. New Brunswick defeated Confederation in 1865, but approved it in 1866. Nova Scotia, in spite of widespread opposition, approved it in 1866. Delegates from the three

The Proclamation of Union. The structure of the Canadian Government is "federal," as is the American. In both nations this type of structure has caused serious problems.

BY THE QUEEN.

A PROCLAMATION

For Uniting the Provinces of Canada, Nova Scotia, and New Brunswick into One Dominion under the Name of CANADA.

VICTORIA R.

WHEREAS by an Act of Parliament passed on the Twenty-ninth Day of March One thousand eight hundred and sixty-seven, in the Thirtieth Year of Our Reign, intituled "An Act for the Union of Canada, Nova Scotia, and New Brunswick, and the "Government thereof, and for Purposes connected therewith," after divers Recitals, it is enacted, that "it shall be lawful for the Queen, by and with the Advice of Her Majesty's most Honorable "Privy Council, to declare by Proclamation that on and after a Day therein appointed, not being "more than Six Months after the passing of this Act, the Provinces of Canada, Nova Scotia, and "New Brunswick shall form and be One Dominion under the Name of Canada, and on and after "that Day those Three Provinces shall form and be One Dominion under that Name accordingly:" And it is thereby further enacted, that "such Persons shall be first summoned to the Senate as "the Queen, by Warrant under Her Majesty's Royal Sign Manual, thinks fit to approve, and "their Names shall be inserted in the Queen's Proclamation of Union:" We therefore, by and with the Advice of Our Privy Council, have thought fit to issue this Our Royal Proclamation, and We do Ordain, Declare, and Command, that on and after the First Day of July One thousand eight hundred and sixty-seven the Provinces of Canada, Nova Scotia, and New Brunswick shall form and be One Dominion under the Name of Canada. And We do further Ordain and Declare, that the Persons whose Names are herein inserted and set forth are the Persons of whom We have, by Warrant under Our Royal Sign Manual, thought fit to approve as the Persons who shall be first summoned to the Senate of Canada.

FOR THE PROVINCE OF ONTARIO.	FOR THE PROVINCE OF QUEBEC.	FOR THE PROVINCE OF NOVA SCOTIA.	FOR THE PROVINCE OF NEW BRUNSWICK.
JOHN HAMILTON,	JAMES LESLIE,	EDWARD KENNY,	AMOS EDWIN BOTSFORD,
RODERICK MATHESON,	ASA BELKNAP FOSTER,	JONATHAN M'CULLY,	EDWARD BARRON CHANDLER,
JOHN ROSS,	JOSEPH NOËL BOSSÉ,	THOMAS D. ARCHIBALD,	JOHN ROBERTSON,
SAMUEL MILLS,	LOUIS A. OLIVIER,	ROBERT B. DICKEY,	ROBERT LEONARD HAZEN,
BENJAMIN SEYMOUR,	JACQUE OLIVIER BUREAU,	JOHN H. ANDERSON,	WILLIAM HUNTER ODELL,
WALTER HAMILTON DICKSON,	CHARLES MALHIOT,	JOHN HOLMES,	DAVID WARK,
JAMES SHAW,	LOUIS RENAUD,	JOHN W. RITCHIE,	WILLIAM HENRY STEEVES,
ADAM JOHNSTON FERGUSON BLAIR,	LUC LETELLIER DE ST. JUST,	BENJAMIN WIER,	WILLIAM TODD,
ALEXANDER CAMPBELL,	ULRIC JOSEPH TESSIER,	JOHN LOCKE,	JOHN FERGUSON,
DAVID CHRISTIE,	JOHN HAMILTON,	CALEB R. BILL,	ROBERT DUNCAN WILMOT,
JAMES COX AIKINS,	CHARLES CORMIER,	JOHN BOURINOT,	ABNER REID M'CLELAN,
DAVID REESOR,	ANTOINE JUCHEREAU DUCHESNAY,	WILLIAM MILLER.	PETER MITCHELL.
ELIJAH LEONARD,	DAVID EDWARD PRICE,		
WILLIAM MACMASTER,	ELZEAR H. J. DUCHESNAY,		
ASA ALLWORTH BURNHAM,	LEANDRE DUMOUCHEL,		
JOHN SIMPSON,	LOUIS LACOSTE,		
JAMES SKEAD,	JOSEPH F. ARMAND,		
DAVID LEWIS MACPHERSON,	CHARLES WILSON,		
GEORGE CRAWFORD,	WILLIAM HENRY CHAFFERS,		
DONALD MACDONALD,	JEAN BAPTISTE GUÉVREMONT,		
OLIVER BLAKE,	JAMES FERRIER,		
BILLA FLINT,	Sir NARCISSE FORTUNAT BELLEAU, Knight,		
WALTER M'CREA,	THOMAS RYAN,		
GEORGE WILLIAM ALLAN.	JOHN SEWELL SANBORN.		

Given at Our Court at Windsor Castle, this Twenty-second Day of May, in the Year of our Lord One thousand eight hundred and sixty-seven, and in the Thirtieth Year of Our Reign.

God save the Queen.

provinces, Canada, New Brunswick and Nova Scotia, went to England in the autumn of 1866, and worked out the details of the bill that passed through the British Parliament, and was given Royal Assent, March 29, 1867, as the British North America Act. This act broke up the Province of Canada into two new provinces, Ontario and Quebec and set up the new government of the Dominion of Canada at Ottawa. It became law on July 1, 1867.

Macdonald was knighted for his work and was asked by the Governor General to form the first government of the new Dominion of Canada. So he was now Sir John A. Macdonald, the Prime Minister of Canada.

All of this was, however, just the beginning. Ultimately Canada was to fall heir to all the British possessions in North America north from the American border to the North Pole; but there was much to do before that was realized. The most pressing problem was what to do about the Hudson's Bay Company. The British government was anxious that the Hudson's Bay Company should turn over its extensive western territories to the new Dominion. Macdonald was not very anxious to accept them, but he felt he had not many options left. "If we don't go there," he said ruefully, "the Yankees will...."

Chapter 6
Bringing in the West, 1868-1871

There was no help for it. The Hudson's Bay Company's rule was dying. Everyone knew it. The Americans certainly did. Their purchase of Alaska from Russia in March 1867, for $7.2 million was only, in their view, a beginning. They would have loved to have gone on and bought out the Hudson's Bay Company had Britain allowed them to. Then there was British Columbia, with only about 28,000 whites, 80,000 First Nations Peoples and some 1,036,000 square kilometres of inviting emptiness. It lay between Washington territory and American Alaska, waiting. Wherever Macdonald looked there were problems. Nova Scotia, now in Confederation, was thoroughly dissatisfied, and would have to be pacified somehow. Newfoundland had to be dealt with. Prince Edward Island, still unconfederated, was talking of making a reciprocity treaty with the United States all on its own.

But at least he had domestic comfort. He was not a widower any more. Along with the British North America Act, he brought a wife home to Canada; he had now, almost for the first time, a real wife and a real home. In February 1867, he married Susan Agnes Bernard, a healthy, handsome, determined woman of thirty years of age, some twenty-two years younger than Macdonald. Macdonald slowed down a bit, and began to enjoy a few creature comforts. He still went on bouts of drinking; he still remained, in fact, rather a man's man; Susan Agnes, for all her determination, did not by any means get all her way, but her influence was continually present, and as a rule this influence was for the better. She was apt to be more partisan than her husband; but one old Liberal who had seen a lot of Macdonald (both good and bad) called Susan Agnes, Macdonald's good angel. Like other good angels she did not always have a good temper, but her instincts were good, and as time went on Macdonald leaned on her more and more. Nevertheless, there is quite a bit we don't know about her. We don't know what Macdonald thought of her. We don't have any of his letters to her. There is an unhappy suspicion that Susan Agnes saw to it that they did not survive. (She died in 1921, thirty years after Macdonald.)

It was not *all* happiness, that marriage. All people have their

Susan Agnes Bernard Macdonald

own private tragedies and Macdonald had already had more than his share. Now, in February 1869, he was to have another, one of the hardest. Agnes gave birth to a disabled and developmentally-delayed daughter, Mary. At first, Macdonald and his wife did not know the whole truth about her condition, but it soon became obvious that Mary would never be able to walk unsupported, and that she would never be fully independent. Macdonald read to her often. She used to write to her father (with the help of her nurse) whenever he was away, asking how soon he'd be home, because she missed him so. Despite her parent's concern, Mary survived both: Macdonald died in 1891, Agnes in 1921, and Mary in 1933.

Macdonald had to have that fundamental toughness and resilience of spirit. He knew that life was not a bed of roses. To some who complained to him about their troubles, he would say, "Do you expect to go through life without difficulties? Be philosophical, and if Fortune empties a chamber pot on your head, just smile and say, 'We are having a summer shower.'"

No, 1869 was not a good year for Macdonald. He was broke, for one thing. And Newfoundland defeated Confederation that autumn. Although various further attempts were made – even a near miss in 1895 – Newfoundland was to remain outside Confederation until 1949. Then came the North-West. Arrangements were made for the acquisition of the Hudson's Bay Company territory, called Rupert's Land. Canada would get it for a song, dirt cheap, at only $1.5 million. The Americans would have paid thirty times as much. The price was not the difficulty. The difficulty was that the people in Rupert's Land, the Métis, did not really want to become Canadians, at least not without any conditions or terms. They wanted some sort of protection for the only way of life they knew. Most of them had been born and raised in the West; it was the only world that mattered to them, that prairie:

...flying shadows, chased by flying light
Into interminable wildernesses,
Flushed with fresh blooms, deep perfumed by the rose,
And murmurous with flower-fed bird and bee.
The deep-grooved bison paths like furrows lay,
Turned by the cloven hoofs of thundering herds
Primeval, and still traveled as of yore.

This is from a poem of
Charles Mair (1838-1927)
called "Tecumseh." Mair
went west in 1868, and later
lived in Prince Albert.

Direct action was easy enough. The Métis were used to organizing themselves. They had had to do it often enough for the buffalo hunt. The Métis were half French-Canadian and half Native American. They were settlers and fur trappers, who had settled along the Red River and Ruperts Land. Under the leadership of Louis Riel, the Métis, seized the only strong point at Red River, Fort Garry, in November 1869, and instituted what they called a Provisional Government. This stopped the Canadian takeover dead in its tracks. Even the new Canadian Lieutenant-Governor was kept out. The Canadians who lived in the Red River, or to the west at Portage la Prairie, did not like the Métis action; but they lacked the experience, the organization, the numbers, or the local sympathy, to do anything effective about it.

Macdonald was thus presented with a *fait accompli*. He did the only sensible thing – he negotiated. In due course Canada received Rupert's Land from the Hudson's Bay Company; Canada kept 99 per cent of it as the North West Territories, and made the remaining 1 per cent –all 25,000 square kilometres of it – less than half the size of Nova Scotia, into the little Province of Manitoba. Indeed, compared with the rest of the North-West, it was the size of a postage stamp. Still, there it was, with all the apparatus of a provincial government, and with a new Lieutenant-Governor, a Nova Scotian, who turned out to be just what was needed. Without a Métis insurrection, there would have been no Province of Manitoba in 1869, or for many years afterward. So the Métis leader, Louis Riel, can really be called the Father of Manitoba.

But – and it is a big but – in the process of establishing and con-solidating his authority, Riel had had someone shot. He had alienat-ed the Canadians at Red River, and imprisoned some of them; all of them were eventually released but one, an Irish-Protestant trouble-maker, who had lived a few years in Ontario, Thomas Scott. He had caused the Métis no end of trouble, had taunted them and abused them. They threatened him. Scott told them they wouldn't dare to shoot him. But they did. Scott was shot by a Métis court-martial, and he was unbelieving almost to the last. Ontario Orangemen then took up the cudgels to avenge Scott, and created terrible mischief both for Riel and Macdonald. The Ontario government did not help matters by offering a $5,000 reward (about $50,000 today) for Scott's murderers. In the circumstances, the best thing was to get Riel to make himself scarce. To make sure that law and order were pre-served, Macdonald sent out a peacekeeping force in the summer of 1870, composed of British regulars and Ontario militia.

Thus did Manitoba enter Confederation on July 15, 1870. So did the North West Territory. In both cases all the land belonged to the Dominion government, with Métis land claims provided for, and land set aside for Métis children.

As the British regulars and the militia were toiling over the ardu-ous canoe route from Fort William to Red River, in the heat of June and July, 1870, the British Columbia delegates arrived in Ottawa, negotiating for the terms of union for the admission of the west coast colony. British Columbia was an imperial domain, stretching 1,200 kilometres north from the 49th parallel, and from the Rockies to the sea –over 900,000 square kilometres of spectacular beauty, with a population of only 28,000 Europeans, and possibly 80,000 Aboriginals. The terms the British Columbians obtained from Ottawa were generous. The British Columbia Legislative Council had asked for a coach road to the East to be started within three years. The delegates thought they would try for a railway. The Canadian government not only accepted the railway, but agreed to start building it within two years of the date of union! The British Columbia delegates returned to British Columbia well pleased with themselves, and with the old "lightning striker," Sir George Cartier. "We must all remember in B.C.," wrote J.W. Trutch, the leader of the delegation, "that to Sir George Cartier and his followers in Lower Canada we owe...the Canadian Pacific Railway."

Why not Macdonald? What was owing to him? Macdonald wasn't there, or wasn't exactly there. He had been struck down without warning, early in May 1870 (after, admittedly, a bout of strenuous drinking, when the Manitoba delegation had completed its work) by the passage of a kidney stone. It had knocked him unconscious. He could not be moved from his office in the East Block. For a time, the doctors feared for his life. But he was not

Amor de Cosmos became the first Premier of British Columbia

dead yet, and eventually in July, after the British Columbia delegates had gone home, Macdonald went to Prince Edward Island to recover. There, amid the green land, red dust, and blue sea, he walked, read, loafed, got his strength back, and even talked a bit of politics with the politicians of the still unconfederated Prince Edward Island. One suspects he talked persuasively of the means by which the Island might be brought into Confederation. So he came back to Ottawa, in September 1870, almost a new man. He looked it and felt it.

Chapter 7

The Pacific Scandal and the Fall of Macdonald, 1871–1873

I t was just as well Macdonald was so healthy. In 1871 he embarked upon one of the least agreeable and most awkward tasks of his career. He went to Washington in March, as a member of a British commission to settle outstanding issues between the United States and Great Britain (and Canada). There were a number of issues that remained from the Civil War, and they were by no means easy. Macdonald's position was unenviable. Britain wanted a

The British High Commissioners, 1871.

Fenian troops as seen by a Canadian cartoonist.

settlement with the United States; the Americans, still truculent whenever they thought about the *Alabama*, wanted to be settled with; Canada was plainly in the middle, her rights to be bargained over, her wishes low on the agenda. Canada had her own grievances against the United States, mainly claims for Fenian raids, in 1866, 1867 and 1870. (The Fenians were American-Irish freebooters who invaded Canada with the aim of helping to free Ireland from British rule.) Canada also had her own wishes, mainly for a Reciprocity Treaty. There had been a successful reciprocal trade treaty with the United States from 1854 to 1866, allowing for free exchange of natural products such as lumber, fish and wheat. Canadians of both political parties wanted it renewed.

Macdonald, as a member of the British delegation, had to watch while the Americans, as is usual in such diplomatic maneuvers, asked too much. Just the year before, Macdonald had quoted in the House of Commons Canning's rhyming dispatch to Holland in 1826:

In matters of commerce the fault of the Dutch
Is giving too little and asking too much.

Macdonald could have said the same of American diplomacy. But that was not all of his difficulty. The British were sufficiently anxious to settle that Macdonald had to be on guard all the time, within his own lines, so to speak, against the British, who seemed ready to give away much of the Canadian position. Macdonald even had to operate like a secret agent behind the backs of his fellow British commissioners to protect himself and Canada. The British attitude was satirized, with some accuracy, by *Grip*, a comic political magazine, a few years later:

Mr. *JONATHAN* – ...*Say neow; J.B. [John Bull], couldn't yew let me have the little critter? [Canada]*

Mr. *BULL* – *No, no! Disintegrate my Hempire? Never (Aside –But, say, hi couldn't let you've him hopenly; happeartices must be saved; but you are gittin' of 'im gradooal, you know.)*

Whatever emerged from Washington was not going to be easy to defend in Canada. And Macdonald would certainly, as a British Commissioner, and as Canadian Prime Minister, have to shoulder full responsibility.

The result could have been worse. The treaty was accepted by the Canadian Parliament in 1872. The San Juan boundary question (the islands in the Strait of Georgia between Vancouver Island and the United States) went to the arbitration of the German Emperor in 1872. The *Alabama* claims went to an arbitration tribunal in Geneva in 1873. The Canadian inshore fisheries went to arbitration in Halifax in 1877. As to the Canadian claims for Fenian damages, the Americans refused to discuss that, and so Britain compensated Canada! Canada did not get a reciprocity treaty in exchange for the inshore fisheries. The Americans refused to give one. Canada got instead some rather useless rights to the American inshore fisheries, and a substantial grant of money from the Halifax arbitration. In fact, the grant was sufficiently large that for a time the American Congress refused to pay it.

American troops on San Juan Island.

The Treaty of Washington did not inaugurate an era of sweetness and light between Canada and the United States, but it began the end of an era of churlishness and darkness. Eulogies for the "undefended border" do not appear until the era of Franklin D. Roosevelt and Mackenzie King, in the 1930's. There were to be plenty more quarrels yet. The fisheries question arose again in 1885, and it was not really solved until 1910; and there was the awful adventure with Teddy Roosevelt in the Alaskan Boundary dispute in 1903. There were to be plenty more quarrels yet. Macdonald to the end of his life never lost his instinctive suspicion of the Americans, nor his capacity to read their politics shrewdly. He never assumed that they were friendly. He had been quite clear, as recently as 1869 and 1870, that behind the agitation in Red River had been some American money, and a great deal of American sympathy. That it did not go further than it did was because Riel, and the Métis, on balance preferred Canada to the United States.

Macdonald had put off Dominion elections as long as possible, but he had to have an election in August and September, 1872. It was a bitterly contested battle, especially in Ontario and Quebec. In Nova Scotia prosperity had undermined opposition to Confederation; the same was true in New Brunswick; but in the two central provinces the Macdonald government had a hard time.

Elections are not fought with prayers, then or now. Money is the sinews of war, and of elections. Macdonald thought he needed a good deal in Ontario, and so did Cartier and Langevin in Quebec. So friends were duly dunned for it. As Cartier delicately put it, "the friends of the government expect to be assisted in the forth coming elections...." This was to a rich and important Montreal businessman, Sir Hugh Allan.

The government had been negotiating with Sir Hugh Allan about the Pacific Railway. That railway was part of the terms of British Columbia's entry into Confederation (dated July 20, 1871), and Macdonald and the government had been anxious to get it underway. Still, it was a very big project; it would take all the capital Allan could get in Montreal and Toronto, and then more in London and New York. Toronto capitalists were interested in the new company being formed, but were jealous of Sir Hugh Allan, and also had good reason to doubt his competence. Macdonald tried to bring the Montreal and Toronto groups together in the summer just before the election, and had managed well enough that he felt justified in believing that a company could be formed, satisfactory to both Toronto and Montreal interests. So Sir Hugh Allan's money was gratefully accepted by Macdonald, Cartier and Co., and the election went vigorously forward. Ample amounts were used, not just to hire

The Pacific Scandal and the Fall of Macdonald, 1871-1873

bands and meeting halls, or print placards, but frankly to bribe the electors. In those days of open voting, the elector stood up at the hustings and said, "I vote for John A. Macdonald!" or whomever the candidate was. If he had been paid $5 to vote that way, the man who had bribed him saw clearly that the vote was delivered.

Macdonald and his friends spent enormous amounts of money in that campaign. They said they had received some $165,000; Allan claimed to have spent more than double that amount. Whatever the amount, there was bribery on a considerable scale both in Ontario and Quebec; and when the election was over, Macdonald had not much to show for it. He had a monumental hangover and some staggering commitments to Sir Hugh Allan. He had lost some sixteen to eighteen seats in Ontario, and another ten in Quebec. Had he not got all six British Columbia seats, the government would have been defeated, so thin was Macdonald's majority.

Then, in the spring of 1873, just when Sir Hugh Allan's Canada Pacific Railway Company was about to launch an appeal in England for funds, Liberal members of the opposition got hold of hard evidence about that money dispensed in the election of 1872 by Sir Hugh. They began their attack in Parliament in April 1873. Macdonald tried to forestall it by appointing a parliamentary committee to investigate, not really knowing how much the opposition knew. With a government majority on the committee the government was reasonably safe. But it was very uneasy, and rightly so. Then the Liberals bought letters stolen from Allan's solicitor's office. On July 18 these were published, to the utter consternation of the government. Three Liberal papers, the Toronto *Globe*, the Montreal *Herald* and the Quebec *L'Evenement* had it all blazoned on their front pages. "I must have another ten thousand... Do not fail me," was one telegram from Macdonald to Allan's solicitor, on August 26, 1872.

This stuff was dynamite. Its publication shook Macdonald to the core. He disappeared completely for ten days; not even Agnes knew where he was. Some Liberal papers cheerfully suggested he had committed suicide. He was *perdu*, as the French say, meaning lost, hiding or drunk, with friends near Quebec. He got hold of himself, and eventually appeared at Ottawa, but he was badly shaken. So was the government, its morality questioned, its leaders blackened. When Parliament opened on October 23, 1873, the government, with that very narrow majority, was just about on the ropes. They held on, hoping against hope; Macdonald, looking as if a feather would knock him over, got up Monday night, November 3, and made a magnificent speech, defending himself and his government. But when Donald Smith, Conservative member for Selkirk,

Sir Hugh Allan

Alexander Mackenzie

Manitoba, went against the government the following evening, it was virtually over. Macdonald and his government resigned on November 5. The Governor General, Lord Dufferin, called on the Liberal leader, Alexander Mackenzie, to form a government. Macdonald was out. Friends and foes alike believed he was finished.

A cartoon from Grip. The Pacific Scandal was the first scandal in Canadian political history. There have been several since.

"WE IN CANADA SEEM TO HAVE LOST ALL IDEA OF JUSTICE, HONOR AND INTEGRITY" - THE MAIL 26TH SEPTEMBER.

Chapter 8
In Opposition, 1874-1878

In January 1874, Mackenzie called a general election. It was the crowning disaster for the Conservatives. Macdonald himself was elected, but for the rest of his followers, the slaughter was terrible. "We have met the enemy," said one follower, "and we are theirs." Rank upon rank had been mowed down. Some Conservatives, like Hector Langevin, did not even run. When the smoke had cleared, all that was left of Macdonald's 106 Conservatives from the 1872 election was a bare 67. Mackenzie had 140 Liberals.

Macdonald thought seriously of resigning as leader. Could the party ever recover with him as leader? It would always be considered, Macdonald felt, as the "charter-sellers'" party, the party that gave the Pacific Railway charter to Sir Hugh Allan in exchange for those election funds. One morning in February or March, 1874, Macdonald brooded his way down Sparks Street, Ottawa, into the offices of the Conservative paper, the *Citizen*. "Boys," he said, "publish an editorial paragraph in today's *Citzen* announcing my resignation of the leadership of the Conservative party." The editor threw down his pen with some vehemence. "Sir John," he replied, "my pen will write no such announcement, nor will it be published in the *Citizen*." Whatever Macdonald's immediate reaction to this may have been – probably he was half-charmed, half-amused – no such announcement was published. And although he continued periodically in the future to make noises about giving up, his followers wanted him to stay on. But of course, he had to have an income. His ministerial salary stopped on November 5, 1873. Macdonald in fact moved to Toronto, and began to pick up the threads of law practice with his partner in Toronto, the firm of Macdonald and Patton. But the party needed him, and this need asserted itself during the year 1875.

Almost inexplicably, the Mackenzie government began to lose by-elections. There were many of them. The election law that Mackenzie passed in 1874 included many electoral reforms. There were stern new measures to prevent bribery at the polls. They allowed an election to be protested, and held again, if bribery could be proved. Most of all, there was the new secret ballot. The ballot changed many things. No longer did the voter have to stand up in front of everybody and say how he voted. Certainly it stripped the crowds at the hustings, the politicians and their hangers-on, of moral (or immoral) control of the voter. The voter could vote as he pleased and no one need ever know.

In 1875 the Conservatives won three by-elections in Quebec and two in Ontario, and vitually repeated the performance in 1876. By the end of 1876, what with by-elections elsewhere, Mackenzie's great majority of 70 was down to something like 42. The truth was that Macdonald had got hold of a policy that promised to put the Conservatives into power: the protective tariff.

Mackenzie had not been responsible for the depression of the 1870's. It had been imported, like so much else, from south of the border, where it had been particularly severe. But its effects on Canada were extremely unpleasant too. The American manufacturing industry had been built up under the shield of the American tariff system. It dated from the Civil War. Their protective tariff system was like a valve. It opened outward all right, to let out the exports, but it closed against imports. So Canadian manufactures had great difficulty getting into the United States; American manufactures, on the other hand, had no difficulty getting into Canada,

Grip, 1876

WANTED---PROTECTION!!

In Opposition, 1874-1878

since Canada had no protective tariff. American goods, in fact, flooded into Canada in 1875, 1876 and 1877, dumped at prices that dismayed both Canadian manufacturers and their workmen. *Grip* put it in the form of a biblical parable:

1. *And the genius GRIP sat on the outskirts of a great city.*
2. *And it came to pass that a great concourse of people appeared out of the city, coming toward him, and they were burdened as for a great journey.*
3. *And GRIP rose and said unto them, 'Oh ye that come from the city, and that journey thence, tell me now the reason of your journey, for ye seem not like ordinary travelers, but like men distressed and driven.'*
4. *And the concourse of people, even of all trades and handicrafts, came nigh unto GRIP and wept before him.*
5. *And they said, 'Let it be known unto our Lord, even unto GRIP.*
6. *That we are men who make steam engines, and who make furniture, and are cunning in the making of boots and shoes, and skilled in all handiwork of brass and copper, and likewise of tin...*
8. *And we did use to make them in this city, and in others, even from the west unto the east, and throughout this country and in all the coasts thereof.*
9. *And lo, it came to pass that cunning men have deluded the rest of the people...*
10. *And have told them to buy foreign goods, even from a far land, and they buy not ours, wherefore thy servants starve...' (November 11, 1876)*

Macdonald's idea of the protective tariff was, patently, all too successful. But why did not the Liberals take it up, if, as some Liberals believed, the country wanted it? The answer was that many Liberals wouldn't have minded going some distance in that direction, but the strongest, and the most persuasive and powerful elements in the Liberal party, including Prime Minister Alexander Mackenzie himself, were very anti-tariff. It was a question of principle with them. In their view the purpose of the Canadian tariff was to raise revenue. Seventy-five per cent of the Dominion government's revenue came from the tariff. But if it was raised higher than its existing level – about 17 per cent – then, as the Liberals saw it, the tariff became a tax on the poor people of the country, upon their tea, their coffee, their woolens and their cottons (all of which they had to import). A higher tariff would benefit the government; it would mean more revenue; but the government, at least the Liberal government, did not want the extra revenue. A higher tariff would help Canadian manufacturers of woolen goods and cotton goods, by helping keep out foreign goods. The Liberals regarded this as pernicious. They thought of a protective tariff as a tax on 95 per cent of the country for the benefit of 5 per cent. The 5 per cent were the manufacturers.

The Conservatives did not see it that way. They argued that a protective tariff would benefit everyone. They said Canadian factories would thrive; Canadian workmen would have work; and Canadian farmers, too, would be protected from American competition, and would sell their Canadian wheat and Canadian oats to Canadian consumers. Macdonald and the Conservatives called this tariff by a wonderful and magnetic name, "The National Policy." It even got shortened, to N.P.:

The farmer sows and reaps his land
And finds his market close at hand,
His wheat, his meat and all complete
To feed the dweller of the city street.
    Cheer boys cheer, for the old N.P.!
    Its work and wages for you and me.
    With peace and plenty blessed are we,
    Cheer boys cheer for the old N.P.
The workman's heart is strong with bread
He hits the nail right on the head
When he votes for the farmer, and the farmer he
Votes for the workman and the old N.P.
    Cheer boys cheer, for the old N.P.!

In practice, of course, the protective tariff was going to be a good deal more complicated than that, but the essence of its appeal to the Canadian public lay in that poem. Mackenzie was to find it difficult to resist.

There was another element in the election that was to take place in September 1878. Alexander Mackenzie's government got Parliament to pass the Canada Temperance Act.

The aim of it was high-minded enough. Canada in the 1870s had as many bars as grocery stores – in Toronto there were more. Every little country town had its bars, some of them decidedly frowsy, often with a clutch of semi-sodden loafers around. Of course there were grand, sumptuous bars in hotels like the Russell at Ottawa or the Windsor in Montreal. Drinking in Canada was on a monumental scale, and not just wine as in Europe. There was very little locally produced wine in Canada. Some beer, indeed, there was, but

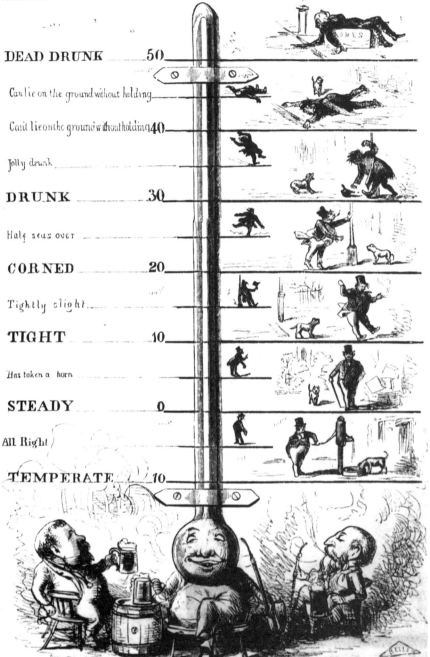

A cartoon from Harper's Magazine, 1860. There was a strong temperance movement in the US at this time, and in other countries as well.

The Inebriometer.

DEAD DRUNK — 50

Can lie on the ground without holding

Can't lie on the ground without holding — 40

Jolly drunk

DRUNK — 30

Half seas over

CORNED — 20

Tightly slight

TIGHT — 10

Has taken a horn

STEADY — 0

All Right

TEMPERATE — 10

In Opposition, 1874-1878

the usual drink was distilled – whisky, gin, or rum. And it was not the "under-proof" watered stuff of today, but real, honest fire-water, that burned with a pale blue-flame, that could rot both guts and morals. Inevitably there were social problems arising from it. So Mackenzie and his government (and, be it said, with very little Conservative opposition), passed in 1878 the Canada Temperance Act, an Act not for nation-wide prohibition, but for prohibition by local option. Each parliamentary constituency could vote in prohibition if it wanted.

It need hardly be said that the distillers, the brewers, and the tavern keepers of Canada took this Act very ill. As one Liberal rue-fully confessed, "every bar in the country became a standing commit-tee room for our opponents." Characteristically, Macdonald had said very little about the bill, for or against. He thought mainly in terms of its political consequences for Mackenzie, and he shrewdly suspect-ed what they might be.

Notwithstanding the Canada Temperance Act, and Macdonald's insistence upon "Canada for Canadians!" (i.e., the National Policy), Mackenzie (and many others), went to the polls on September 17, 1878, fully believing the Government would be returned. Mackenzie was not only surprised at the result, he was devastated. And bitter. One hundred and forty-two seats to the Conservatives and only 64 to the Liberals. The Canadian people preferred wicked Johnnie Macdonald to honest Sandy Mackenzie. The thing was not believ-able! *Grip* remarked that it would have been better for Mackenzie had he worked less hard as Minister of Public Works, and done a lit-tle more wining and dining, or "poking bartenders in the ribs, jovial-ly, like John A... But he could never be taught these little arts...There was no gin and talk about MAC..."

He resigned on October 8, 1878, and the next day Macdonald was asked to form a government. Sir John and the Conservatives, as one Toronto paper remarked, had the look of people who were going to be in office for a long time. Macdonald was in fact going to be Prime Minister until he died.

Chapter 9
Macdonald, the Saskatchewan Rebellion, and the C.P.R., 1878–1885

He began by going to Halifax to meet Lord Lorne, the new Governor General who arrived by sea in November 1878. Macdonald had to heave himself out of bed at Government House, very unsteadily, to go through with it. Lord Lorne's wife was the Princess Louise, a daughter of Queen Victoria. She was quite as imperious as her mother, with most of her mother's temper and some of her looks. Princess Louise found Canadian society generally odious and frequently vulgar. One worthy senator at a Rideau Hall ball, doubtless with a bit too much to drink, was said to have placed his arm familiarly on the vice-regal shoulders and congratulated the Princess on the plumpness of her figure. She was *not* amused. The interest of Princess Louise in Canada was limited to whatever she

Hector Langevin

considered her duty, but was fundamentally what she would have felt in visiting the Colonies anywhere – that is, it was confined to the picturesque. Her relations with Macdonald are best described as strained, for he had a Scottish distrust, and a Canadian dislike, for arrogance and pomposity.

Macdonald's principal lieutenants were to be with him a long time. Hector Langevin was back in the House of Commons as Minister of Public Works, a competent, patient administrator. He was devoted to Macdonald, but without flair, and he never could seem to master the general business of the House. Langevin would also be mortally jealous of Adolphe Chapleau, who was to become Secretary of State in 1882 after having been Premier of Quebec. There was J. H. Pope, Macdonald's Minister of Agriculture, from

Compton in the Eastern Townships of Quebec, a salty, tough, realistic politician, who knew a lot about railways, and was probably closer to Macdonald than any of the other ministers. Macdonald liked to have those kind of men about him – decisive, able, knowledgeable, who knew their own minds and were not afraid to speak them. John Thompson, of Halifax, who came in 1885, was in this respect like Pope. There was also that other Nova Scotian, Charles Tupper, who became Macdonald's Minister of Railways in 1879. Tupper was a tremendous power to the government, bold as brass and twice as loud. Tupper could be counted on to defend, or to oppose, just about anything on five minutes' notice. He had bullying instincts that all governments find handy to use from time to time, especially when the opposition are onto something.

Charles Tupper

Macdonald himself was neither decisive like Pope, nor bold like Tupper. He had physical courage, but politically speaking he could be both indecisive and timid. He disliked change. He thought most changes improved very little. So he disliked bold policies, almost instinctively. Most of Macdonald's most striking political departures were hammered out of the heat of opposition, or by the threat of being put there. In this sense, he was the prototype of Canadian prime ministers since, Laurier and Mackenzie King being the most obvious examples. As he grew older these qualities of his became more obvious, and to some of his old colleagues, decidedly less agreeable. For Alexander Campbell, his Minister of Justice, working with Macdonald became, in 1884 and 1885, a positive irritation.

By that time much had happened. Macdonald was seventy years old in 1885, and at that age a man is entitled to follow old and well-established habits of thought and action. But there were weaknesses, too, and Macdonald, although aware of them, was probably not always able to measure their full effects.

Macdonald himself had taken the important portfolio of the Department of the Interior in 1878. He was also the Superintendent-General of Indian Affairs. He believed that the West was going to be so important that only the Prime Minster should look after it, that the prime ministership should be united, so to speak, with the developing edge of the country. There was much to commend in such a view. Mackenzie, however, had been so pre-occupied with his work as Minister of Public Works, that he tended to neglect his role as Prime Minister. Macdonald did not intend to do that. With Macdonald, it was the other way round. His role as Minister of the Interior was sacrificed to his role as Prime Minister. No doubt Macdonald had his priorities right; but it did mean that the Ministry of the Interior was not administered as it ought to have been.

One has also the impression that the character and the problems of the West rather eluded Macdonald. He had never been west. The furthest he had travelled (up until July 1886, when he went west for the first time), had been when he was nearly drowned in a ship-wreck on Lake Huron in 1859. He never quite understood western-ers, or the conditions that made even easterners who moved there behave like them. He believed most westerners were just out after a fast buck. Here his favorite word was "speculators." And while this perception was no doubt true some of the time, it misrepresents the nature of western agitation. The westerners found their problems very real and pre-sent, and they found the Ottawa bureaucracy, and the local extensions of it, extra-ordinarily slow and difficult to deal with.

Nor was Macdonald much better with Indian Affairs. Here, busy as he was, he probably put too much reliance upon his senior deputy minister, Lawrence Vankoughnet, and not enough upon knowledgeable subordinates in the field. For the Aboriginals had real problems after 1880. The buffalo were being killed off at a speed that no one could believe. They thought the buffalo had just gone some-where and would turn up in their old numbers soon. The buffalo never did. The old

Macdonald in 1883

name for Regina was Pile o' Bones Creek; that was where the buffalo had gone, and the Winchester repeating rifle was largely responsible. The Plains First Nations – the Blackfoots, the Plains Crees, and others – had promises from the Dominion government, by virtue of Treaties No. 6 and No. 7, to supply them with food should the buffalo and all else fail. But the Indian Affairs Department, itself squeezed by the Dominion deficit on current account in 1883 and 1884, cut down the rations and altered their character. Aboriginals were in extremely bad shape by 1884, bitter and resentful.

There had been a hard frost in September 1883 in a number of places on the prairies, and the harvest was badly damaged. In 1884 the trouble was too much rain. The areas most affected by both conditions were the valleys of the North and the South Saskatchewan Rivers west and south of Prince Albert. It was there that trouble broke out in 1885.

The Europeans, Métis, and Aboriginals all had grievances, some in common, some different. They all seemed to get nowhere with Ottawa. They had no M.P.s. (That was to come in 1887.) All they had was the North-West Territories Council, or the ubiquitous petitions that seemed to disappear into Ottawa without leaving a trace. So a combination of disgruntled people in the South and North Saskatchewan sent for Louis Riel.

Riel in the 1880's.

At that time Riel was teaching school in Montana. He was now an American citizen, had married a Métis woman, and had two children. But this call – brought by Métis horsemen all the way from Saskatchewan – deeply stirred the elements within Riel that had once made him shine as a brilliant and egocentric agitator. He would do for the Saskatchewan country in 1884 what he had done for Manitoba in 1869. He did not intend to lead a rebellion; he did not intend anything in the way of armed demonstration; but he would focus western grievances and get redress for them.

There was nothing secret in all of this. Riel moved himself and his family to the Saskatchewan country in early July, and felt out the political ground slowly. He had the general support of the district. Macdonald was told about it all by the Lieutenant-Governor of the North-West Territories, Edgar Dewdney, and it proved accurate.

Gabriel Dumont

Riel made use of the opportunity, "to further his own private ends." But Dewdney added, "if the half-breed question is arranged this winter, it will settle the whole business; if not, a good force in the North[-West] will be necessary." This information was contained in a letter to Macdonald, September 19, 1884.

Macdonald did not like it all much, but he did not think it would come to anything. Westerners were specialists in making a lot of noise about not very much. He had even had intimations by Christmas that Riel could be bought off. In Macdonald's view this confirmed his suspicion that the whole agitation was a scheme to extract money from the Dominion government, either for Riel personally or for the Métis as a group. Perhaps it was. But even so, there were real grievances behind it. Now, early in 1885, was the worst time, when whatever was in the barns from the last September's harvest was running thin, when the Aboriginals were restless and sullen, and when the Métis were growing impatient. For nothing was happening in Ottawa. It was true that the government decided on January 28, 1885, that a commission of three would be appointed to investigate the Métis' land claims in the Saskatchewan. But it was narrowly conceived, and in any case it would be weeks before it started, and months before it finished. Besides, commissions like that had been promised before. Sir Hector Langevin, the Minister of Public Works, had been in Regina in August 1884, and had never even come north to talk to the Métis people. They had waited for several days, watched the roads from the south for the great man who never came. Now, Gabriel Dumont, Riel's senior lieutenant, and a man respected by all who knew him, came to Riel and told him that he had done no good, that the Canadian government would only give in before the threat of sterner measures. "I assure you," Riel told a clergyman later, "that three weeks before the Duck Lake fight [March 26] I had no idea of rebellion." Even the rebellion he did mount was intended as armed blackmail. He knew he could not defeat the Canadian government. But, though Riel had extensive Aboriginal support, especially after Duck Lake, he lacked the skill and the communications to handle their help. And he did not have support from two important groups who had substantially helped him in 1869. For one, the English-speaking Métis would not take up arms. While sympathetic to Riel and his cause, they had not bargained for rebellion. Secondly, the church would not support him. He was now too extreme for the local priests, in thought and in deed. Too convinced of his own communication with God, and too headlong in action, he had soon outdistanced, and even on occasion threatened, Father André of Prince Albert, Father Fourmond of St. Laurent, and Father Moulin at Batoche, all of whom opposed, in varying degrees, Riel's measures.

Riel's Saskatchewan rebellion was put down by a Canadian volunteer and militia army and by the Mounted Police. It cost the Canadian government about $5 million. Perhaps it might have been better to have handed out $5,000 in order to get Riel out of the country, and to have settled the Métis claims in some decent fashion. As it was, the legacy of Riel was to linger a long time. The jury at his trial in Regina in July 1885, had said he was guilty, but recommended mercy. The jury knew that Riel was as sinned against as sinning. Riel, during all these months, was almost certainly mad, by any modern definition. But it was not then the legal definition. Macdonald was determined that this time there was going to be neither mercy nor

Lord Strathcona at Craigellachie, November 7, 1885.

Troops arriving in Winnipeg on the CPR, 1885.

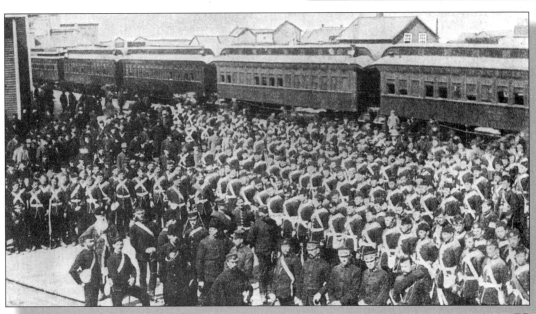

George E. Foster

pardon. Macdonald used to follow jury recommendations for mercy; but Riel was hanged, Monday, November 16, 1885.

Just nine days before the unhappy event in the Regina jail, the C.P.R. drove the last spike of the railway at Craigellachie, in Eagle Pass, east of Kamloops. Macdonald had needed the C.P.R. to transport troops west to the Saskatchewan rebellion. Now it was the government's turn to give something. The railway badly needed a government loan. They had had one in 1884, but the enormous costs of construction had quite swallowed it up. The government advanced a second loan in June 1885, in the teeth of strong opposition in the Conservative caucus, to say nothing of opposition in Parliament. It took a good deal of blackmailing all round to settle it. Thus, the Saskatchewan rebellion saved the C.P.R. Macdonald, that old master of tactics, had set one problem neatly to offset another. As tactics, this was masterly. As effective government, however, it was frankly desperate. And Macdonald knew it.

His cabinet was, by 1885, pretty much a wreck. Macdonald seemed to be doing all the work, and he was seventy. Sir Leonard Tilley wanted out, being desperately unwell; too many others of the cabinet were old, or tired, or ill, or all three together. Macdonald needed new blood desperately. He ought to have had it long before this; the western crisis now drove him into a major effort. He succeeded in getting three good new ministers in 1885. In August, Thomas White, of Montreal, became Minister of the Interior, and was soon to win golden opinions in the West. In September, John S. D. Thompson, of Halifax, became Minister of Justice, and was soon the real workhorse of the Macdonald government. In December, G. E. Foster, of Fredericton, New Brunswick, a classics master, who looked a paragon of probity, became Minister of Marine, then Finance. Thus when the storm broke as a result of the hanging of Riel, the Conservative ship was braced and equipped to meet it.

Chapter 10
The Last Years, 1886–1891

Macdonald handled the parliamentary side of the Riel agitation neatly. When Parliament met, late in February 1886, the government arranged the debate so that it focused on one question: whether Riel ought to have been hanged. The debate did not turn, as it probably should have, on the inefficiency of the government that had caused the rebellion, though it was impossible to keep that out of the debate. Laurier put it neatly: "Had they [the government] taken as much pains to do right, as they have taken to punish wrong...the law would never have been violated at all." The result was that both parties split, on almost a free vote, with the Liberals getting the worst of it. (In the vote, 146 M.P.s supported the proposition that Riel should have been executed; 23 of these were Ontario Liberals. Only 52 M.P.s regretted Riel's execution, of whom 15 were French-Canadian Conservatives.) The plain fact was that even with a powerful issue like the Saskatchewan Rebellion, the opposition was simply outmaneuvered by the Macdonald government.

Edward Blake

It was not quite so easy with the Quebec public, where there was a great deal of criticism of Macdonald and the government for the hanging of Riel. In October 1886 the Quebec Liberals under Honoré Mercier won a narrow victory in a provincial election. So Quebec began 1887 with its second Liberal regime since 1867, and the first one of any solidity. That was owing to Riel as much as to any single issue.

The Liberals also won in Nova Scotia, in a provincial election in June 1886, called on the issue of the repeal of Confederation. It looked very much as if Macdonald's government, notwithstanding its new cabinet ministers, might have difficulty when it had to go to the polls in 1887.

Macdonald called a Dominion election at the beginning of 1887, and all of this provincial

Wilfrid Laurier

agitation against Ottawa seemed to come to naught. There were Liberal premiers in the four eastern provinces – in Nova Scotia, New Brunswick, Quebec and Ontario – but they could not seem to stop Macdonald. Notwithstanding all that could be said against Macdonald, his methods and his government, he won the general election of February 22, 1887, with a comfortable majority of 37. This majority was not the big majority of 68 after the election of June 1882; but that Macdonald won at all in 1887 was remarkable.

Edward Blake, the leader of the Liberal party, took it all very badly. He had been leader since 1880, had fought two elections, and lost both. In June 1887 he resigned. Macdonald was sorry to see Blake go; he felt he could go on beating him election after election. Blake was exceptionally able, talented and hard-working. But he was too much a one-man show. His leadership lacked warmth, or even the appearance of warmth. He lacked the instinct of how to develop and hold the loyalties of his party. He would occasionally sleep during speeches of some Liberals. Macdonald rarely, if ever, did that to his followers. Wilfrid Laurier became the new Liberal leader.

Laurier was very different from Blake. Blake was an intellectual, with a massive, strong, encyclopedic mind; at the same time he was tense, neurotic and self-centered. Laurier was an actor at heart, gifted with intelligence, poetry, charm, and – essential for political life – courage. Blake had been a bear for work: Laurier avoided it. Blake knew finance and business well: Laurier knew almost nothing about it. Blake tended to operate by his brains, Laurier by his instincts.

Laurier became leader about the time when a wave of religious passions, especially among Protestants, made life for both political parties difficult. Macdonald himself had never taken kindly to racial or religious passion of any kind. Macdonald was brought up a Presbyterian, but he went frequently to the Church of England and was by now too wise (or too cynical) to believe that any Christian denomination had a monopoly of ways to Heaven. Macdonald cabinets contained Protestant Irishmen and Catholic Irishmen, French Roman Catholics, Scotch Presbyterians, drinkers and teetotalers – in fact representative of the wide spectrum of the Conservative party itself. The Liberals were not that much different, though they did tend more to a Protestant-Ontario orientation. Basically, both parties had to be Catholic and Protestant at the same time, and they were. It was impossible that a Canadian political party, in a country 40 per cent Roman Catholic, 30 per cent French, be anything else but an amalgam. That did not prevent extremists in both camps from making life difficult. One celebrated example of this was the Jesuits' Estates Act.

This Act settled a long and tangled controversy in the Province of Quebec. The Church grumbled but accepted the settlement. The Quebec Protestants accepted it. But Honoré Mercier, the Quebec Premier, trailed a long preamble to the Act, with correspondence to and from the Pope, almost, one suspects, as a bait for Ontario Protestants, who had been so outspoken against Riel in 1885. In any case, the Ontario Protestants reacted. Soon the Protestant drums were beating all over Ontario against the wickedness of a Canadian provincial government having official relations with the Pope. They insisted that the Act be disallowed, as the Ottawa government had the power to do.

Macdonald had no intention of touching the Act. His reaction to the Protestant call to arms was entirely characteristic. He let other Conservatives in Parliament attack the motion for disallowance on the grounds of principle, that such a motion was divisive, pernicious, un-Canadian. Macdonald himself fell back on an old story, as he so frequently did. Many a time in the past he had put off stern Liberal criticisms of his policies with a story that had grown old and comfortable in his service. This time it was about a Jew who had ordered a ham sandwich (strictly against his religion) in a restaurant, and was about to eat it, when a ferocious thunderstorm broke outside and lightning flashed at the restaurant windows. The Jew said, "All that fuss about just a bit of ham!" So, too, said Macdonald, the Jesuits' Estates Act.

Like an old sweater or an old jacket, Macdonald's stories were put on whenever Macdonald wanted to get Parliament down off its high horse. You could get at human beings better with laughter than with passion. Many were the times when Macdonald's humor dissolved tension in the House and restored it to sanity and common sense. In 1883 Blake made one of his complaining speeches, saying that the Speech from the Throne had painted much too bright a picture of Canada, and what was needed was appropriate doses of gloom. Macdonald said,

My honorable friend puts me much in mind of an old Newcastle collier who had been boxing the compass for many years....

After a visit of seven years to the West Indies he came back to England, and when his ship was approaching the land, and when he felt the familiar sleet and storm and saw the familiar clouds, he put on his sou' wester and his peajacket and said: "This is something like weather; none of your infernal blue skies for me."

In 1887 the Liberals sought their own version of tropical skies. They invented a new policy for Canadian trade with the United States. They called it Commercial Union. It meant what it said. It would sweep away the Canadian-American tariff border, and set up a common collectivity of tariffs with the United States, not unlike the present European Common Market. Some Americans, including some congressmen, made sympathetic noises. The Americans liked the word "union" in the phrase "commercial union." It seemed to point to political union. The Liberals tried to say they only meant "commercial" union. But it was not easy; the more the Americans expressed a liking for it, the more difficult became the position of the Liberals in Canada. They were in fact forced, early in 1888, to change the name, to "unrestricted reciprocity." That new expression was a mouthful to begin with. And it was not the same thing as commercial union. Nor did the Americans like it. Nevertheless, it appealed to a considerable section of the Liberal voters. It was roughly what they wanted. Realistic it was not: popular it was. This would not be the first, nor the last, time that a substantial section of the Canadian public has swallowed medicine that was useless but tasty.

Macdonald and the Conservatives were not opposed to reciprocity. A standing offer of reciprocity had been incorporated as part of the National Policy tariff of 1879. But it was limited to the kind of reciprocity British North Americans had had with the United States from 1854 to 1866, – that is, in natural products, such as fish, wood, fur, wheat, milk. Macdonald had tried in 1871 to get that in exchange for the fisheries. The Americans wouldn't touch it. And while in 1890 the Americans were more sympathetic, there was no real hope for the kind of reciprocity that Conservatives could have accepted.

Early in 1891, Sir John Macdonald decided to dissolve Parliament. There would be a general election. One was due, in any case, before March 1892. There were good reasons not to wait. One was the Langevin scandal. Sir Hector Langevin had been Minister of Public Works since 1879. Trouble was brewing, storm clouds were gathering on the horizon and Macdonald did not like the look of it. Privately to Macdonald, Langevin denied any wrong doing, but certain revelations implicated Langevin's department in the old, familiar political game – kickbacks. The Department would award a contract by tender to firm X. Firm X would pay some of the profit of the contract to a favored M.P., in this case Hector Langevin's friend and relation, Thomas McGreevy, member for Quebec West. By the autumn of 1890 Langevin himself was being accused. There is some suspicion that Macdonald wanted an election before too much of that scandal broke into the open.

The second reason for dissolution was the only one that Macdonald could use in the campaign. This

"THEN AND NOW"

Grip, 1888. A reminder that Macdonald had changed his position on reciprocity– supporting it in the 1850's but opposing it in the 1880's.

was the discovery of the Farrer pamphlet. Edward Farrer was a Liberal, a writer for the Toronto *Globe*, the great Liberal paper; he was brilliant, clever, and unprincipled. An American friend wanted to know the best way, commercially, to drive Canada into the arms of the United States. Farrer obligingly set down to write such a pamphlet and had it privately printed. The printer gave the proof sheets to the Conservatives. It was dynamite. It could blast open the whole trade policy of the Liberals. It was not very nice politics – (so the Governor General told Macdonald) but much is fair in politics.

So Macdonald went after the Liberals. They were, he said, disloyal. They were traitors. They were secretly thinking of annexing Canada to the United States. The Conservatives issued posters showing the Liberal leaders, Laurier and Cartwright, the editor of the *Globe*, conferring with the President of the United States,

THE OLD FLAG.
THE OLD POLICY.
THE OLD LEADER.

Benjamin Harrison, on how best to arrange and divide up the "Canadian states." Against that the Conservatives showed Macdonald, supported on the shoulders of a farmer and laborer, carrying the Canadian flag, with the motto, "The old flag, the old policy, the old leader." Macdonald himself made his famous declaration on Canadian nationality:

As for myself, my course is clear. A British subject I was born – a British subject I will die. With my utmost effort, with my latest breath, will I oppose "veiled treason" which attempts by sordid means and mercenary proffers to lure people from their allegiance....

It was powerful stuff, that election appeal. Though the times in the early 1890's were not easy, Macdonald won the election of March 5, 1891. He was to remain in power till the end of his life. It was not, however, the 38-seat majority he had won in 1887, but a narrower 27-seat one, and here his edge came mainly from support in Nova Scotia and New Brunswick. He broke about even in Ontario; Laurier had given him a close run in Quebec.

And it had been a hard campaign. Winter campaigns usually are, more especially so then. Joseph Pope, Macdonald's secretary, described him ill in bed one bleak February afternoon in Kingston:

Sir John stayed with Dr. Williamson, his brother-in-law, a widower who lived in a desolate-looking house with the minimum of comforts of any kind, painfully lacking the evidence of a woman's touch, and was besieged by politicians who thought only of their immediate interests, intent only on extracting from him the last measure of service. "Joe," said Sir John to me one afternoon as he lay half dozing in his cheerless room, "If you would know the depth of meanness of human nature, you have got to be a Prime Minister running a general election!"

The 1891 session of the new Parliament opened late in April. Many new faces were present, many that Macdonald had not seen before. He had recovered from his February illness and was his usual jaunty self again. Or he appeared to be. One old Liberal crossed the floor to shake hands with Macdonald one day in May, inquiring after his health. "My dear fellow," said Macdonald with a sad smile, "I feel I shall not be troubling you for very long." Nor was Laurier deceived. He had the feeling an old institution in the land was gradually sinking. However, it has to be said that Pope had rarely seen Macdonald in better form than at the familiar Saturday night dinner at Earnscliffe on May 24. But that was the last. A few days later, Macdonald was hit with a massive stroke that at once deprived him of all speech; he never really recovered from that. He died quietly on Saturday, June 6, 1891, at 10:30 in the evening. He was seventy-six years old.

Macdonald's greatness lay in so many things, it is quite unnecessary to cover up his failings. He was a vigorous, at times shameless, partisan. He believed in the Conservative party, and what it could do for Canada. He believed in ensuring, so far as he could, its

Earnscliff, Macdonald's home in Ottawa

The funeral procession of Sir John A. Macdonald leaving Parliament Hill

continued rule. He also bullied the provinces. He assumed that the Dominion government, at least when it was Conservative, knew what was right for the country. He was never particularly scrupulous when it came to winning victories, either for the Dominion government or the party. Nevertheless, all that being said, Sir John A. Macdonald was a great man. He was always after realities. He was impatient with mere words, or with mere appearances. His cynicism – if that is the word for that shrewd skepticism of his – was the astringent necessary to clear the lens of his mind, in order to focus it sharply on men and on issues as they really were.

His mind was of a rare kind: when seized, albeit reluctantly, of the necessity of change, Macdonald was extraordinarily skilful at devising ways to effect it. Best of all, his mind had a remarkable range. He read everything he could get his hands on. And he remembered what he read: biography, history, letters, novels, all were sifted into that capacious and versatile mind of his. The truth is, as you may discover for yourself, he was, and he still is, wonderful company.

Macdonald in 1888

Further Reading

The standard biographies of the main figures in the text are:

Careless, J. M. S. *Brown of the Globe*, vol II. Toronto: Macmillan, 1963.

Creighton, Donald G. *John A. Macdonald.* Toronto: Macmillan, 1952-55, 2 vols.

Stanley, George. *Louis Riel.* Toronto: Ryerson, 1963

Thomson, Dale. *Alexander Mackenzie: Clear Grit.* Toronto: Macmillan, 1960

The most valuable contemporary account of Macdonald is the memoirs of his colleague and personal secretary from 1881 onwards:

Pope, Maurice, ed. *Public Servant: The Memoirs of Sir Joseph Pope*, Toronto, Oxford, 1960.

Other general works about the period:

Careless, J. M. S. *The Union of the Canadas: the growth of Canadian institutions, 1841-1857* Toronto: McClelland & Steward, 1967

Morton, W. L. *The critical years: the Union of British North America, 1857-1873* Toronto: McClelland & Stewart, 1964

Waite, P. B. *Canada 1874-1896: Arduous Destiny,* Toronto: McClelland and Stewart, 1971

Waite, P. B. *The Life and Times of Confederation, 1864 -7* Toronto: University of Toronto Press, 1962

Waite, P. B. *Macdonald, His Life and World.* Toronto: McGraw-Hill, Ryerson, 1975.

Credits

The publishers wish to express their gratitude to the following who have given permission to use copyrighted illustrations in this book:

British Columbia Archives, pages 33, 36
Manitoba Archives, page 31
Metropolitan Toronto Library Board, pages 3, 4, 8, 12, 14, 19, 21, 23, 27, 28, 30, 35, 38, 40, 41, 43, 44, 46, 55, 59, 60
Ontario Archives, pages 4, 7
Parks Canada, page 13
Public Archives of Canada, pages 5, 10, 11, 15, 17, 18, 24-5, 34, 48, 49, 50, 51, 52, 53, 54, 56, 61, 62, 63

Index